Journal Three

Seasons of Hope

M. Donna MacLeod

Ave Maria Press AVE Notre Dame, Indiana

To Erynne Lee MacLeod,
a cherished daughter who loved Jesus
and now lives with him,
and
to her dad, my dear husband Bryan,
who has faithfully been by my side
every step of this life-giving ministry.

Paperback: ISBN-13 978-1-64680-235-7

E-book: ISBN-13 978-1-64680-279-1

Cover and text design by Katherine Robinson.

Printed and bound in the United States of America.

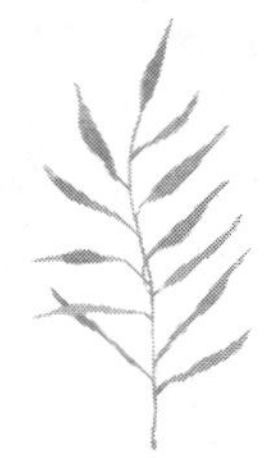

Contents

The Seasons of Hope Prayer can be easily found on the back cover of this book.

Welcome to
Seasons of Hope Journal Three

Dear Brothers and Sisters in Christ Jesus,

When your loved one went home to the Lord, did you think that God was calling you to a new life in him, too? And that this new life held much more than pain and sorrow?

I had no idea what lay ahead when my daughter Erynne died. Years of caring for the dying and their families as a nurse did not prepare me for my own grief. Yet God would use the lessons I learned for the good of others. From the loss of a precious child, a Christ-centered ministry to the bereaved and a hospice were born. God plans ahead. He didn't forget me, my family, or my community, and he hasn't forgotten you. He wants to console you.

Trusting in God and opening your mind and soul to the Seasons of Hope program blesses you in untold ways. Your broken heart will start to mend as your spirit lifts. I've seen it happen time and again.

Perhaps this *Journal* reached you through the kindness of a concerned friend who knew its mini-retreats with Jesus could ease your sorrow. Or maybe you found all four of the program journals on your own and plan to use them each day or once a week until the sessions are finished. Or you may have wanted to attend a Seasons of Hope group at church but couldn't, so someone from the ministry team sent you a *Journal* and possibly offered to call you each week to support your efforts.

Most likely though, you have this *Journal* because you joined a Seasons of Hope group that meets at church or online. You might be attending for the first time. Or you might have a season or two under your belt and are back for more. You realize that the support of others who know what you are going through will once more bless your grief journey with God's gift of love.

Whether you use the *Journals* independently or have group support, you are a vital part of this powerful ministry. Grounded in scripture and the healing wisdom, traditions, and practices of the Catholic Church, Seasons of Hope truly focuses on faith and the spiritual side of grieving. In the midst of suffering, it can draw you ever closer to the Lord. What a gift from heaven that is!

A *Journal* and a Bible are all you need for group sessions or independent journaling. You begin each week with the Seasons of Hope Prayer, located on the back cover of this *Journal*. Then you turn to a new Guidepost page for the title, theme, and scripture citation to locate the Bible passage that guides the session. On the next page you will find the Marking the Route activity that draws from the scripture's theme. The adjoining Notes page has space to write your thoughts related to the exercise.

If you attend a group, the facilitator will have faith-sharing questions based on the session's scripture story for you and the other participants to consider. And you also enrich your weekly journey with the *Journal*'s retreat-like Soul Work that you do at home after the session.

If you are a journaler, you read the session's Bible story and do the Marking the Route exercises plus soothe the wounds of your heart and soul with the Soul Work. The process generally take about twenty minutes, a commitment that most schedules can handle.

The Soul Work's theme and opening comments in Looking Back offer a fresh way to view the scripture story. You then ask for guidance in A Prayer to Find the Way. You will read Steps along the Path to learn how the scripture story relates to mourning and then spend time with the Reflection section to consider your situation. You

can write your thoughts in the space provided under the heading Journal Entry.

To help you cope, Moving Forward offers a Church tradition or act of charity that generates hope. You finish the Soul Work with the Closing Prayer to thank God for the gift of consolation.

The appendix at the end of the booklet has some treasures of its own. Are you interested in literature and websites about losing a loved one? Check out Helpful Resources, which also includes links to sacred images used for contemplation in some sessions. Are you in a group? Use the Network Directory to record contact information about your new friends in Christ. How about ground rules for the group? That's covered in the Guide to Group Etiquette. Want to help your facilitators plan for the next season? The Season Survey lets you formally share your ideas.

By using this *Seasons of Hope Journal Three*, you bring the trials of your loss to the Lord. You embrace his teachings, reflect on your loss, and share the painful moments so that your wounded spirit can grow strong in him.

May Seasons of Hope's unique way of placing Jesus Christ at the center of your grief bring you consolation and healing.

In Christ our Hope,
M. Donna MacLeod

Guidepost: Point of Departure

Theme: Believing

Scripture: John 20:24–29

Marking the Route

Exercise:

The way we respond to news surrounding the loss of someone is rooted in our family of origin's ideas and rules about death. This exercise visits the past. Please complete these statements:

- My name is____.

- The first family member whose death I recall was my__________ ____, who died when I was______________years old.

- The rules about dealing with death that I remember from childhood are . . .

- The person who laid down the rules was . . .

- The rules taught me that God . . .

Notes

Soul Work: Point of Departure

Looking Back: *Doubting Thomas*

This session we see why one of Jesus's disciples was tagged with the unenviable name of "Doubting Thomas." Some would argue that Thomas's reaction in John 20:24–29 is appropriate. After all, his brethren are claiming that Jesus is alive after his Crucifixion and death. The grieving disciples sound like they have lost their minds.

Did Thomas forget that Jesus had foretold his death and Resurrection? Or had witnessing Christ's Passion and death weakened the disciple's belief in him? What we know is that Jesus believes in Thomas. He understands grief, his followers, and their limitations. Addressing Thomas's doubt directly, Jesus offers his holy wounds for Thomas to probe so that Thomas will believe. He uses Thomas's shaken faith to send a message of healing to all who struggle to believe in him during mourning.

Instead of inflicting more pain on the Lord by touching his wounds, Thomas sees and believes and says, "My Lord and my God!" Some call those words the most explicit statement of faith in the New Testament. Thomas shows us that saints don't have to be perfect. They simply must love God.

A Prayer to Find the Way

O merciful Savior,
in the troubled moments
since losing my loved one,
I have been afraid of many things.
Yet, like Thomas,
my love for you remains.
Through your kindness,
may the gift of faith
guide me through mourning.
Amen.

Steps along the Path

Who hasn't had a moment of doubt after losing a loved one? Be comforted in knowing that when the resurrected Jesus finally encountered Thomas, he greeted him and the other mourners with "Peace be with you." The Prince of Peace didn't want their hearts to be troubled or afraid, so he came to them.

During this time of sorrow, have you thought about the many ways the Prince of Peace is present to you?

Reflection

One way to encounter Christ is to focus on an image of his sacred wounds. A picture of the crucified Christ from a book or prayer card will do, or you can sit before a crucifix in a church or chapel where you can gaze at a life-size figure. The wounds on Christ's hands, feet, and side represent the Lord's selfless act of love for all the saints and sinners of the ages.

Journal Entry

As Christians, we live with the expectation that when our time comes to an end, we will meet face to face. Sometimes being at the side of a dying loved one forces us to wrestle with our own mortality. That's perfectly normal. Also, when we mourn the loss of a loved one, thoughts about life after death may arise.

Write down your thoughts about life after death. If you need a little help getting the words down, consider these opening phrases:

Lord, losing_________________makes me realize . . .

My connection to_________________has shown me that life is . . .

❧ Moving Forward

Jesus surrounded himself with ordinary people with human weaknesses and gave them the means to be holy. Since the eleventh century, the Church has canonized saints to show heroic virtue worthy of public veneration.

Yet we are all called to lead holy lives. Living saints are simply all those who live according to the law God has given us. Our family members, friends, and those who dedicate their lives to God are saints among us every day.

This week honor your loved one by a visit to his or her grave or place of internment. While you are there, remember something he or she used to do that reminds you of Christ.

Closing Prayer

O Savior of my soul,
with a grateful heart I thank you
for the gift of my departed loved one.
Strengthen my faith and let me
recognize your face
as we walk this journey of sorrow
together.
Amen.

Session 2

Guidepost: Path to Understanding

Theme: Knock and the Door Shall Be Opened
Scripture: Matthew 7:7–11

Marking the Route

Exercise:

Jesus wants to be invited into your sorrow, so he will knock at your door. When you open the door of your heart to him, you have taken the first step toward healing.

Conjure up an image in your mind's eye of Jesus at your door. Sketch him or write down a description of what you see. While you're at it, ask Jesus for something you want that will ease your grief.

Notes

Soul Work: Path to Understanding

Looking Back: *Open Doors*

Matthew 7:7–11 gives us a sense of how Jesus admires the kindness of God the Father. The Lord assures us that all prayers receive attention and are answered in the most loving manner. Yet the sorrow of losing a loved one may cause us to pause at that notion. Haven't we prayed for a cure for someone for relief of their pain or for God to rescue them from the jaws of death? And how often has the answer been no?

Jesus is adamant, though: "Ask, and it will be given you; search, and you will find." Is he telling us to seek truth? Can we ever break free of our tunnel vision and get a glimpse of God's wisdom?

A Prayer to Find the Way

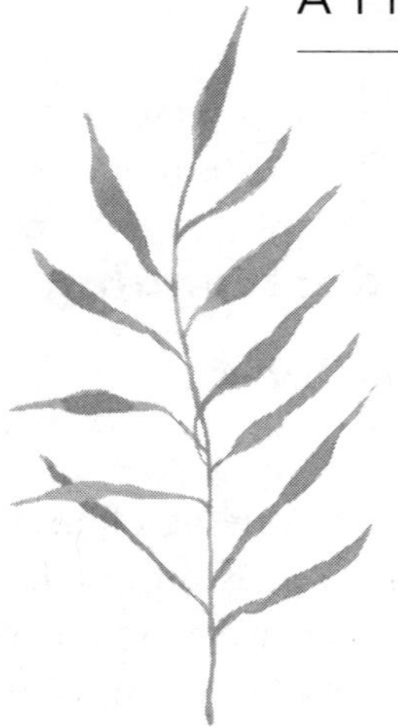

O merciful Savior,
you teach us about God the Father's
infinite love and wisdom.
Let us discover him through you
as the door of consolation opens for us.
Amen.

Steps along the Path

Sometimes after a loss, grief is so confusing you may forget that God wants to console you. When you find it difficult to concentrate, to organize your thoughts, or to remember the simplest things, how can you pray? A wandering mind can't fully comprehend the message of a scripture passage, either. Once the initial confusion wears off, the impact of the loss may leave you deaf and blind to God's presence in your sorrow.

When you knock on God's door with prayer, do you recognize his reply? Quiet your own thoughts and listen attentively to what comes to mind. Try to imagine your request from God's perspective. For whose will to be done do you pray?

Jesus promises that our heavenly Father's gifts exceed our expectations and that his way is the way of perfect love and wisdom. His door opens to those who seek him.

Reflection

Jesus spent much of his ministry explaining the nature of God the Father and the loving regard he has for his creation. Your attitude toward God influences how you pray. Is it as expectant and trusting as Jesus recommends? Do you wonder if you are heard or whether the door of mercy will open for you? Reflect on your relationship with God. The better you know him, the better you will see God acting in your life. What do you think God's will is for you during these difficult days?

Journal Entry

In Matthew's account, Jesus speaks confidently about God the Father's desire to answer our prayers. Trust is the underlying issue. Jesus calls upon us to accept his advice and rely on his character, ability, strength, and truthfulness.

Write to Jesus about your trust in him and how it affects your prayer life, especially when doors need to be opened in times of trial.

Moving Forward

The path to understanding grief takes you past many entrances that promise spiritual growth. Attending a Christ-centered support group such as Seasons of Hope can map the way. You get to choose which door to knock on.

To knock takes a deliberate act on your part. One way to grow in the Spirit is to stop by the doors of the tabernacle at your church. The sacred place of reservation that holds the hosts consecrated during Mass gives constant access to the presence of the Lord Jesus. The posture you assume (whether you kneel or sit in reverent attentiveness) will convey your heartfelt message to him as well.

If possible, spend quiet time in front of the tabernacle this week. Let your prayer knock for you, and expect the door of understanding to open wide.

Closing Prayer

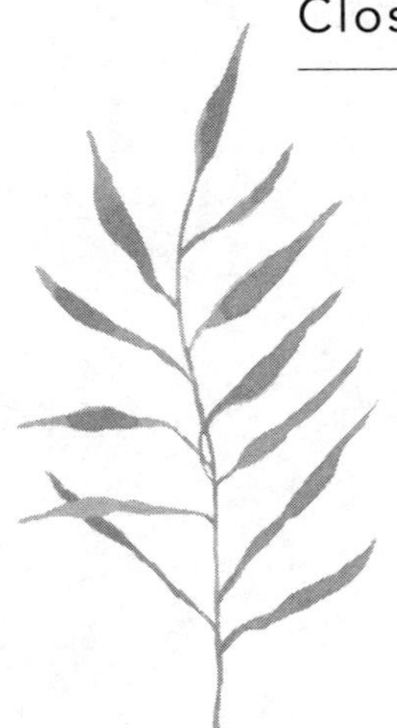

Lord Jesus,
your words of encouragement
bring peace to my weary heart.
I'm grateful for the doors you open
for me.
Amen.

Guidepost: Obstacles on the Journey

Theme: Our Infirmities

Scripture: Luke 13:10–13

Marking the Route

Exercise:
Like the woman in Luke's gospel who was unable to stand erect, we get weighed down by carrying the heavy burden of our grief. Others may see how burdened we are, but only the Lord knows how to lighten our load. Think about how it will feel when the Lord heals your wounded spirit. Jot down your thoughts.

Notes

Soul Work: Obstacles on the Journey

Looking Back: *Crippled Spirit*

The backdrop for the story of Luke 13:10–13 contributes to its drama. It is the Sabbath, the seventh day of the week in the Hebrew calendar. Observed from Friday evening to Saturday evening, it is set aside for worship and rest from ordinary everyday activity. Jesus is at a synagogue, a house of worship, where his brethren gather for the public reading of scripture, prayer and the sacrifice of praise, and instruction on religious matters.

After the reading, it was common for a synagogue leader to invite someone who was particularly qualified to speak to the congregation. That may be why Jesus was teaching that day before a crowd which included a synagogue leader.

Jesus spots a woman who is crippled so badly she cannot stand erect. Modern medicine might view her condition as a chronic sprained back, but the divinity of Jesus rightly discerns the woman's wounded spirit. Even today, humanity's affliction and infirmity are a fertile testing ground for the faithful in need of Jesus's healing.

A Prayer to Find the Way

O Jesus, healer of my soul,
sometimes it feels as if
I am like the woman weighed down
and wounded in spirit.
I ask you to set me free of my
affliction—
the heavy burden of mourning.
Amen.

Steps along the Path

Worry commonly accompanies grief. Uncertainty about the future may make you wonder whether you can handle life without your loved one. So many plans and dreams wrap around a relationship. Feeling uneasy or apprehensive is a normal emotional response to such a loss. The peace you seek, however, goes beyond feelings. It is rooted in the soul.

In the scripture story, the woman's ailment seemed physical in nature, but it required spiritual healing. As a person of faith, she joined in communal worship and most likely had prayed for God's help for many years. Jesus also must have prayed with the congregation before healing her.

When he saw the crippled woman, he addressed her and declared that she was set free of her problem. Scripture doesn't share her thoughts. Did she realize that her prayer was answered? Was she listening to Jesus? Or was she deaf to his voice?

Jesus laid his hands on her, touching her with the Holy Spirit, which brings wholeness to body, mind, heart, soul, will, intellect, and emotion. Jesus, the first charismatic healer of the Church, showed the woman and all humanity his saving power.

Reflection

The woman's response to her healing was dramatic. She immediately stood up straight and glorified God. Can you imagine how she must have felt? Did she dance about and shout? Did she laugh or cry? Did she embrace the Lord or fall at his feet?

What would you do in her situation? What do you do when Jesus touches your sorrow?

Journal Entry

The crippled woman found a solution to her problem at an unex-
pected moment. God seems to work that way. Write to Jesus about
what cripples your spirit these days and get ready for a reply.

Moving Forward

When you reflect on your spiritual growth during mourning, it helps to consider how Christlike you are in carrying your cross.

Sometimes sorrow makes it difficult to pray and listen to God's message. Normal grief can bring a variety of confusing reactions, such as sadness, anger, anxiety, guilt, and self-reproach. These feelings may foster everyday faults (venial sins) that weaken spiritual health. The Sacrament of Penance and Reconciliation is a powerful way to seek healing.

When you welcome peace, serenity of conscience, and spiritual consolation through the sacrament, God touches you. So stand erect in faith and glorify him!

Closing Prayer

O healer of my soul,
with grateful heart
I receive the gifts of your Church
and the sacraments that bring me
ever closer to you.
Thank you for guiding me
toward health of body, mind, and spirit.
Amen.

Session 4

Guidepost: Path to Inner Healing

Theme: Blinders to Faith
Scripture: Luke 18:35–43

Marking the Route

Exercise:

Think about the scene from Luke's gospel that depicts the blind man's encounter with Jesus. What strikes you most about the story?

Take the next few minutes to write a letter to God about how you are like or unlike the blind man as you call upon Jesus to ease your suffering. Ask for something that will help you get through the grieving process.

Notes

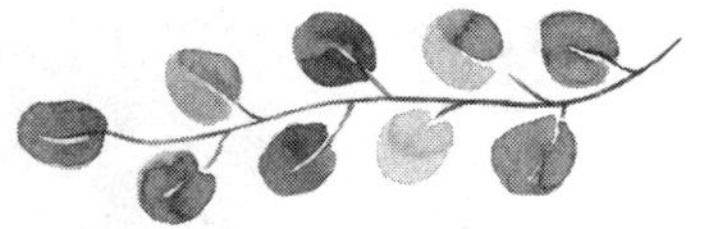

Soul Work: Path to Inner Healing

Looking Back: *Blind Faith*

The story in Luke 18:35–43 opens as Jesus and a group of followers approach the town of Jericho nestled in the oasis of the Jordan Valley.

A blind man begging by the roadside wonders what is happening and questions the strangers passing by. When he learns that Jesus of Nazareth is near, he shouts out and begs Jesus to have mercy on him. In a protective reaction that the disciples resort to time and again, those walking in front rebuke the man and insist that he be silent. Could these disciples be the Twelve?

The blind beggar calls out all the more, addressing Jesus as the Son of David. This title indicates his belief that Jesus is the Messiah—the one anointed by God's Spirit. The covenant of the Hebrew people was known to have several anointed ones of the Lord, particularly King David, who lived about one thousand years before Jesus. The Israelites, such as the blind beggar, hoped for the coming of a king, a son of David, who would bring salvation.

The blind beggar's shouts draw Jesus's attention. The Lord stops and has the crowd bring the blind man forward, involving them in the miracle about to unfold. Surely, Jesus knows what the man wants, but he asks the man to get more specific than "have mercy on me." How often in your grief have you sought Jesus's help and forgotten to be specific?

A Prayer to Find the Way

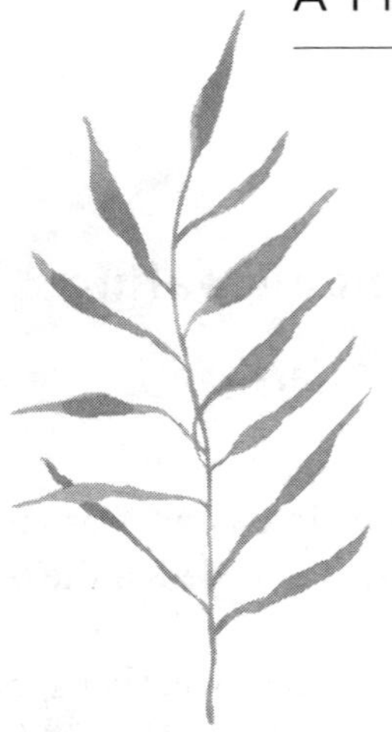

O compassionate Savior,
I am in need of your pity, too.
Sometimes I'm left by the roadside
as life passes by,
and I do not know that you are near.
Be the Lord of my life,
and I will no longer be blind.
Amen.

Steps along the Path

When the pain of losing someone consumes every waking thought, it debilitates as surely as the blindness the beggar endured. We can learn much from the beggar's attitude. Notice that once Jesus spoke to him, the man addressed him as "Lord," which acknowledges Jesus's transcendence and dominion over humanity.

We can only wonder if Jesus chose this humble soul at this particular point on the way to Jerusalem to show his disciples what blind faith accomplishes. The message is the same today.

Reflection

Jesus fulfilled one of the characteristics of being the messiah by bringing good tidings to the afflicted beggar. Jesus also was sent to bind up the brokenhearted.

Have you called upon the Lord's mercy to gain healing? Have you begged? According to the dictionary, a beggar is simply a person who lives by asking for gifts.

Journal Entry

God knows and provides for your every need. Yet Jesus sought the beggar's input and granted his wish. Take time to think about what would ease the pain of your grief and explain it to Jesus in the space below.

Moving Forward

Scripture gives us only a peek at some of Jesus's compassionate acts. He never seemed to mind interruptions or being approached by complete strangers. A walk down a country road prompted actions that inspire the ages.

This week, be inspired. Look for an opportunity to help someone in need of compassion. If you want to imitate our Lord, expect him to put someone needy in your path. Just keep your eyes open!

Closing Prayer

Dear Lord,
your consolation gives me the strength
to get beyond my sorrow.
Thank you for the opportunity to
grow in spirit this week.
Amen.

Guidepost: Way of Suffering

Theme: His Wound of Love
Scripture: 1 Peter 2:20b–24

Marking the Route

Exercise:

The image of the Sacred Heart of Jesus on display in group, on a prayer card, or posted online guides our exercise today.

Gaze at the image of the Sacred Heart and observe the wound inflicted as Jesus hung lifelessly on the Cross. Imagine the burst of blood and water that flowed out as symbols of his love—the Precious Blood of the Eucharist and the holy waters of Baptism. Think about Jesus's desire to share his heartfelt love, grace, and healing with you now. Write to him about what comes to mind.

Note: For the next session, have an item with you that reminds you of the faith of your loved one.

Notes

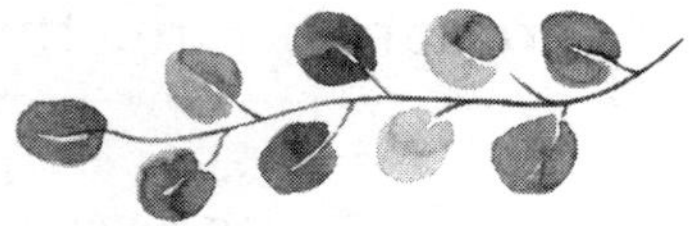

Soul Work: Way of Suffering

Looking Back: *Christ's Example*

People have always needed reassurance in times of suffering. The passages from Peter's letter (1 Pt 2:20b–24) to members of the early church explore suffering in light of Jesus's example. The Lord's phenomenal courage was worthy of imitation back then and is just as meaningful today. It models how faithful followers confront trials of all kinds, including mourning a loved one.

Peter's letter tells us to be like Jesus—to place God's will first and accept that suffering fosters spiritual growth. Yet who greets a painful turn of events with open arms? Not most of us. We feel betrayed. We grumble. We are more human than holy.

When you suffer a loss without complaint, Peter's writing suggests that such patience is a grace before God. God has given you the ability to respond to his call to new life in him (salvation). This favor of God is not earned or deserved; it's a gift.

A Prayer to Find the Way

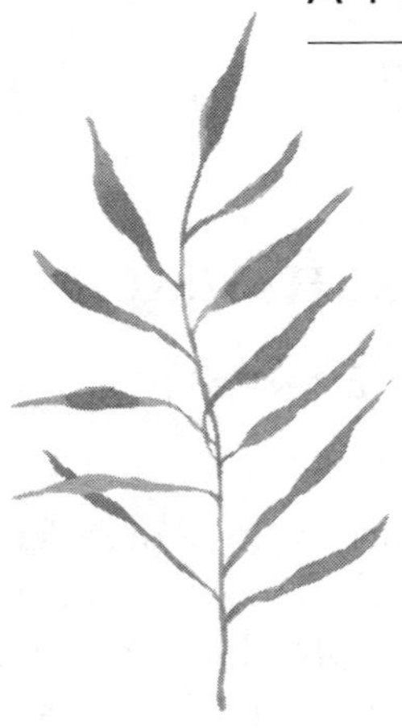

O suffering Savior,
you so loved the world
that you chose to suffer and die
out of love for us.
One day we will be with you in a
place that knows no sorrow.
Be my faithful companion on the
road of mourning.
Amen.

Steps along the Path

The scripture passage reminds us of the call to follow in Jesus's footsteps. Yet the emotions of grieving often bring out the worst in us. When someone you love dies, you may wrestle with regrets or missed opportunities. You may beat yourself up over the past or simply feel that life beat you up. Do you wonder if you did something to deserve the pain? That's normal. Feeling guilty is a manifestation of grief.

Remember that bad things do happen to good people. Jesus himself faced unthinkable trials, but his response was love. The benevolence of our God was revealed through him.

Reflection

When Mother Teresa of Calcutta was called a "living saint," she would smile knowingly. She saw God in everyone but especially in those who suffer.

Think about your departed loved one and how his or her life reflected God to you and others.

Jesus handled the trials that came his way. He was sinless and honest, returned no insults, accepted suffering, submitted himself to judgment, and obeyed God's will.

When have you followed in his footsteps on your road of suffering? Write to Jesus about your situation.

Moving Forward

Sorrow can weaken your body, emotional outlook, and spirit, but don't despair. Food strengthens the body and attitude while the Eucharist strengthens the spirit. Christ is present for us in the Blessed Sacrament. It is a sacred sign of grace that Christ wants to share with you.

If you attend Mass and receive the Eucharist as often as possible, expect your life to change. Through communion with Jesus, you learn to truly love God, let go of your miseries, and grow stronger in faith. You will sense his desire to console you in your grief. The saints have testified to this, as do everyday Catholics who receive Communion frequently. The next time you receive the Eucharist, ask Jesus to give you courage in these hard times.

Closing Prayer

O Jesus,
you are the source of all consolation.
I am grateful to discover you in the
midst of my suffering.
Let me receive you in the Eucharist
with an open heart
and trust completely in you.
Amen.

Session 6

Guidepost: Final Destination

Theme: Do Not Weep

Scripture: Luke 7:11–17

Marking the Route

Exercise (for a group member):
Show the group something that reminds you of the faith of your departed loved one and tell why it's special to you.

Exercise (for a journaler):
At each session, you have honored your deceased loved one with word and prayer. Today, go a step further. Consider the item you selected for this session that reminds you of the faith of your loved one. Write about why it is special to you.

Note: Seasons of Hope *has four different seasons. Find out when the next one starts.*

Notes

Soul Work: Final Destination

Looking Back: *No Tears*

The final scripture reading of this season (Lk 7:11–17) testifies to the power of Jesus to change lives even when hope seems lost. Accompanied by his disciples and a large crowd, Jesus is on the way to a town about five miles southeast of Nazareth. At the town gate, they meet a funeral procession of impressive size.

Throughout history, Jewish people have attached great importance to the burial of a loved one. Scripture identifies the bereaved as a widow, a noteworthy point in light of her son's death. If she had no other children, she would have been without support and left to the charity of the community.

The tears of the grieving widow touch the Lord's heart, and he is moved with pity for her. We can only guess what he is thinking. Does he foresee the plight of his own mother before his eyes? Or does he envision this widow as the embodiment of all those who grieve?

Jesus also attends to the deceased son, who sits up on the funeral bier at his command. Jesus doesn't stop at restoring the young man's life; he gives the young man to his mother. The reaction of everyone, including the reunited family, is awe and praise of God.

Steps along the Path

You have probably met someone who refuses to attend funerals. These people sometimes fear the reality and finality of death in general. Some are afraid to express thoughts and feelings about the deceased. Others let their absence make a statement about their relationship with the deceased or bereaved family.

On the other hand, Jesus is ever present to those who mourn. This story about the raising of the widow's son is but one example of his mercy. Today he embraces the brokenhearted through his Church and its funeral rites.

Reflection

Thinking about the funeral or memorial service of your loved one may still bring tears to your eyes, but it is worth contemplating. Compare the emotions displayed during the funeral procession in the gospel to what you experienced.

Journal Entry

Whether or not you were physically present to your loved one at the time of death, you likely remember your last moments together. Write to Jesus about how he was also present in those moments and now in your memories of them.

Moving Forward

If Jesus hadn't brought the young man back to life, the widow would have observed the Jewish customs that dictate distinct periods of mourning. Special observances would have been conducted the first week. A certain prayer that affirms faith in the wisdom of God's decree would have been recited daily. A memorial service would have been held on the thirtieth day, and a general period of mourning would have lasted for eleven months.

Our Church also remembers its faithful. In some parishes, it is common for a Mass intention to be offered a month after the funeral. Although Mass intentions can be arranged at any time, those who die within the year are often honored at a communal remembrance celebration in November. Request that a Mass be celebrated in memory of your loved one. Jesus will be there.

Closing Prayer

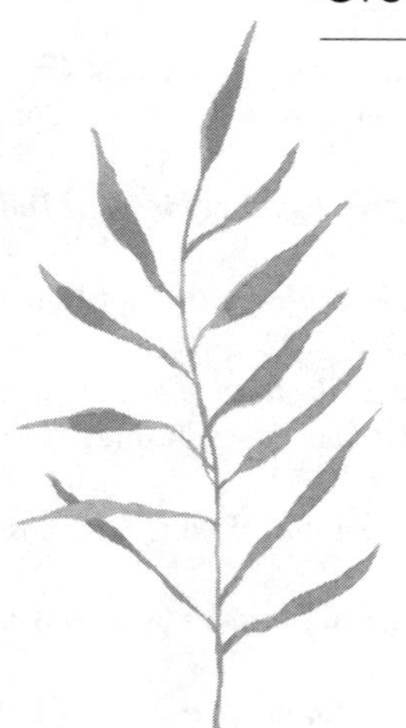

O merciful Jesus,
you comfort me in moments of
sorrow and weeping.
Thank you for once again
wiping away my tears.
Amen.

Appendix

Helpful Resources

Books

DeLorenzo, Leonard J. *Our Faithful Departed: Where They Are and Why It Matters.* Notre Dame, IN: Ave Maria Press, 2022.

Gilbert, Richard B. *Finding Your Way after Your Parent Dies: Hope for Grieving Adults.* Notre Dame, IN: Ave Maria Press, 1999.

Helping Children Cope with Death. Portland: Dougy Center, 2015.

Helping Teens Cope with Death. Portland: Dougy Center, 2015.

Hickman, Martha Whitmore. *Healing After Loss: Daily Meditations for Working Through Grief.* New York: Avon Books, 1994.

Kübler-Ross, Elisabeth, and David Kessler. *On Grief and Grieving: Finding the Meaning of Grief through the Five Stages of Loss.* New York: Scribner, 2005.

Lafser, Christine O'Keeffe. *An Empty Cradle, a Full Heart: Reflections for Mothers and Fathers after Miscarriage, Stillbirth, or Infant Death.* Chicago: Loyola Press, 1998.

Noel, Brook, and Pamela D. Blair. *I Wasn't Ready to Say Goodbye: Surviving, Coping, and Healing after the Sudden Death of a Loved One.* Naperville, IL: Sourcebooks, 2008.

Nouwen, Henri J. M. *Turn My Mourning into Dancing: Finding Hope in Hard Times.* Nashville: Thomas Nelson, 2001.

O'Connor, Mary-Frances. *The Grieving Brain: The Surprising Science of How We Learn from Love and Loss.* New York: Harper One, 2022.

O'Hearn, Patrick, Bryan Feger, Kelly and Ryan Breaux. *The Grief of Dads: Support and Hope for Catholic Fathers Navigating Child Loss.* Notre Dame, IN: Ave Maria Press, 2023.

Roe, Gary. *Comfort for the Grieving Parent's Heart: Hope and Healing After Losing Your Child.* Cleveland: Healing Resources, 2020.

Rowland, Joanna. *The Memory Box: A Book about Grief.* Illustrations by Thea Baker. Minneapolis: Sparkhouse Family, 2017.

Rupp, Joyce. *Now That You've Gone Home: Courage and Comfort for Times of Grief.* Notre Dame, IN: Ave Maria Press, 2009.

Shoener, Ed, and John P. Dolan, eds. *When a Loved One Dies by Suicide: Comfort, Hope, and Healing for Grieving Catholics.* Notre Dame, IN: Ave Maria Press, 2020.

Tighe, Tommy. *St. Dymphna's Playbook: A Catholic Guide to Finding Mental and Emotional Well-Being.* Notre Dame, IN: Ave Maria Press, 2021.

White, Michael, and Tom Corcoran. *Seriously, God? Making Sense of Life Not Making Sense.* Notre Dame, IN: Ave Maria Press, 2021.

Wolfelt, Alan. *Understanding Your Grief: Ten Essential Touchstones for Finding Hope and Healing Your Heart.* Fort Collins, CO: Companion Press, 2021.

Zonnebelt-Smeege, Susan J., and Robert C. De Vries. *Getting to the Other Side of Grief: Overcoming the Loss of a Spouse.* Grand Rapids, MI: Baker Books, 2019.

Websites

www.bible.usccb.org/bible provides free access to the New American Bible.

www.hospicefoundation.org has a treasure trove of articles on grief and grieving.

www.whatsyourgrief.com offers grief and bereavement education and social media resources for adults, teens, and children.

www.widowedparent.org supports widowed mothers and fathers with children in the home.

www.avemariapress.com has books on prayer, bereavement, and spiritual enrichment.

www.compassionatefriends.org offers information and support for families who lose a child.

www.grasphelp.org supports those who have lost a loved one through the misuse of drugs.

www.healgrief.org provides grief resources, virtual groups, educational programs, and a map to find local and national support.

www.samaritanshope.org links to information on suicide-survivor issues for all ages.

www.taps.org helps those grieving the death of a military loved one by providing free grief resources, including casework, counseling, publications, retreats, seminars, and more.

Sacred Images

"Divine Mercy," www.thedivinemercy.org/message.

"Rosary," https://rosarycenter.org/how-to-pray-the-rosary.

"Sacred Heart of Jesus," https://m.theholyrosary.org/sacredheart/.

"Stations of the Cross," https://aleteia.org/2018/03/30/pray-the-stations-of-the-cross-with-these-beautiful-images-and-prayers/.

Network Directory

Interacting with others of faith who understand what it means to lose a loved one gives you a chance to give and receive support. Use the space below for contact information of participants in your Seasons of Hope group.

Name____

Phone number_______________________________________

Email____

Name____

Phone number_______________________________________

Email____

Name____

Phone number_______________________________________

Email____

Name____

Phone number_______________________________________

Email____

Name____

Phone number____

Email____

Name____

Phone number____

Email____

Name____

Phone number____

Email____

Name____

Phone number____

Email____

Name____

Phone number____

Email____

Guide to Group Etiquette

A facilitator guides the faith-sharing process by keeping the focus on the Lord and the session questions. A facilitator doesn't teach, preach, or advise. The facilitator creates a safe place for you to talk about your feelings about loss and receive consolation.

You are expected to

- come each week and make it known if you can't;

- arrive on time;

- treat others with respect;

- share your faith story and then let others talk;

- be a good listener;

- keep what is shared in confidence; and

- be open to God touching you through others.

Don't worry if tears flow. They are part of grieving. Smiles and laughter are welcome, too.

Season Survey

Please take a few moments to complete the statements below about your experience with our Seasons of Hope group. Thank you!

1. I learned about Seasons of Hope from

2. I think the meeting room is

3. For me, the session start time is

4. For me, the length of the weekly sessions is

5. The focus on prayer, scripture, and God is

6. Private time to write, listen to music, or read allows me to

7. I find faith sharing

8. For me, the fellowship break is

9. Soul Work between sessions lets me

10. What I learned from Seasons of Hope is

11. When the next Seasons of Hope group forms, I

12. I'd also like to say

Date: ____

Name (optional): ____

Acknowledgments

How grateful I am to God for the blessing of so many who made this updated edition of the Seasons of Hope *Leader's Guide* and *Journals* possible. Only God can make goodness flow from the sorrow we bear. And I truly believe the Seasons of Hope program embodied in these books is a powerful witness to that reality.

My heartfelt thanks remain with the clergy, family, friends, and bereaved who believed long ago that this work would enrich our parishes. They were right! I'm also grateful to everyone who lifts us up in prayer and to the brokenhearted who trust in the Lord and come to be comforted. I appreciate the priests, deacons, religious sisters and brothers, lay pastoral advisors, and diocesan leaders that welcome the program. And I admire the amazing Seasons of Hope facilitators and helpers, at my side and everywhere else, who have faithfully poured their gifts, talents, and compassion into season after season of this Catholic grief-support ministry. Their feedback is woven into this edition.

The ongoing enthusiasm and expertise of the Ave Maria Press professionals and staff are greatly appreciated. Many thanks especially to Eileen Ponder, Karey Circosta, Erin Pierce, and Stephanie Sibal for championing this new edition.

As always, my husband Bryan's wisdom, love, faith, and generous spirit greatly influenced this work. I treasure the input of our dear daughter Meganne, who remains a constant source of love and support, and the memory of our dear Erynne, whose death opened my heart to all who mourn.

M. Donna MacLeod is a Catholic leader and founder of the Seasons of Hope ministry to the bereaved. She is the author of the program's bestselling *Leader's Guide* and four companion journals. This work was inspired by the loss of her youngest daughter, Erynne, in 1988 and the compassionate response of her parish.

MacLeod holds bachelor's and master's degrees in nursing and has served as an oncology clinical specialist, nurse educator, administrator, and hospice professional. She served on the board of trustees and training faculty of the former National Catholic Ministry to the Bereaved and is a member of the Catholic Family Life Association.

Macleod delivers keynotes, workshops, retreats, and other presentations online and at numerous national and diocesan conferences and parish events related to grief, loss, and ministry leadership in the United States and Canada. A seasoned ministry mentor, MacLeod supports Seasons of Hope facilitators with online resources and an enrichment series sponsored by Ave Maria Press. She also leads parish Seasons of Hope groups in the Diocese of Fall River, Massachusetts

She lives with her husband, Bryan, in the Boston, Massachusetts, area. She can be reached at seasonsofhope35@gmail.com.

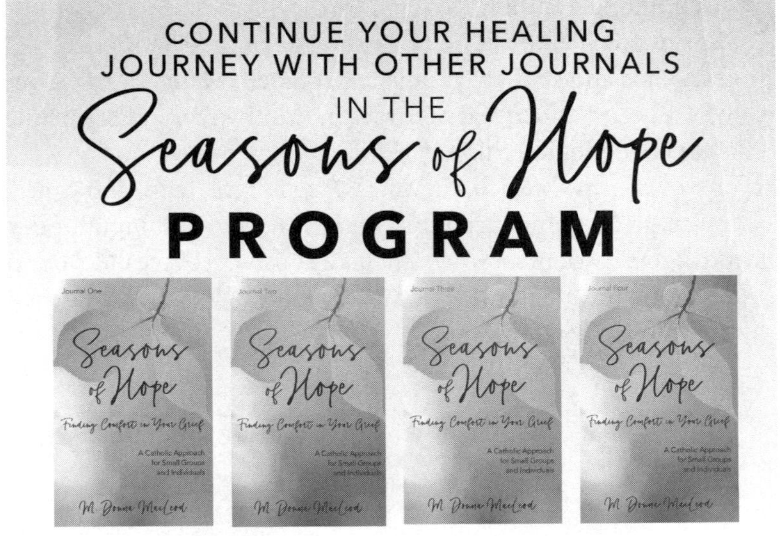

Each journal covers a unique, six-part, standalone season of six sessions that have their own themes.

Look for these titles wherever books and ebooks are sold.